I0134042

Rusted Bells and Daisy Baskets

poems by

Andrea Panzeca

Finishing Line Press
Georgetown, Kentucky

Rusted Bells and Daisy Baskets

Copyright © 2016 by Andrea Panzeca
ISBN 978-1-944899-54-7 First Edition
All rights reserved under International and Pan-American Copyright Conventions.
No part of this book may be reproduced in any manner whatsoever without written
permission from the publisher, except in the case of brief quotations embodied in critical
articles and reviews.

ACKNOWLEDGMENTS

"One More Time for Pelican Drive" won the 2012 UNO Vassar Miller Poetry Award
(judge Shara McCallum), and top honorable mention for the 2012 Andrea Saunders
Gereighty/Academy of American Poets Poetry Award (judge Julie Kane). It appeared in
Ellipsis, vol. 39.
"Smoking Outside with My Cat on Sunday Morning" appeared in *Ellipsis*, vol. 41.
"The Infinite Santa Monica Sand" won the 2013 Andrea Saunders Gereighty/Academy of
American Poets Poetry Award (judge William Virgil Davis). It appeared in *Ellipsis*, vol. 40.
"Floating in the Pool" won the 2013 UNO Vassar Miller Poetry Award (judge Shelley
Puhak). It appeared in *Ellipsis*, vol. 40.

This book would not be possible without Martha & Robert Panzeca, Mike & Corinne
LeClaire, Frani & the Shafers Wes Darian & Gavin, BJ & Nikole Jones, Brian & Michael
Hendrickson, the Martins, the Menishes, the Soniats, Bunny Rabbit, Wilma Pretus, Jim
Hahn, Jenny Probus, David Greenwell, Travis Benton, Daniel Schleith, Tiffany McBride,
Tamberly Ammons, Lauren Caulfield, Alicia Tuttle, Angel Kellem, Karen Turner, Brent
Hagan, Matt Gilmour, Tuni, Rusty, Suzy, Skippy, Lucy, Pinky, Nico, Sya, Cutty, and so
many more yet to name.

Also much gratitude to Barbara Hamby, Erin Belieu, Brigitte Byrd, John Gery, Carolyn
Hembree, Randy Bates, Elizabeth Steeby, Jeff Shotts, Julie Ezelle Patton, Adam Fitzgerald,
Ben Morris, Kelly Jones, Liz Hogan, Carrie Chappell, Roxy Seay, Nordette Adams, M.E.
Riley, Megan Burns, Desireé Dallagiacomo, Maritza Mercado-Narcisse, LaJana Paige, the
staff at ACA, and all my fellow artists along the way.

Publisher: Leah Maines
Editor: Christen Kincaid
Cover Art: Martha Panzeca
Author Photo: T. L. McBride
Cover Design: Elizabeth Maines

Printed in the USA on acid-free paper.
Order online: www.finishinglinepress.com
also available on amazon.com

Author inquiries and mail orders:
Finishing Line Press
P. O. Box 1626
Georgetown, Kentucky 40324
U. S. A.

Table of Contents

for Jessica Sandoval & Megan Eldridge

"paradise gave me these legs / for spinning"

—Jane Mead, "Paradise Consists of Forty-Nine
Rotating Spheres" from *The Lord and the General Din
of the World*

One More Time for Pelican Drive

Thank you greatly God almighty, You put me in my place, in central Florida
on Merritt Island—like a one-island archipelago connected by a torso.

I look at maps like porno mags. But You had plans for me; kept all those falling
rocket boosters from landing on me, gave Frani the disposition to ignore her little

sister when I would want to wrangle (or "make smoke" as I called it, like fights
in *Looney Tunes*). My neighborhood was active. We almost had Olympics

to rival Barcelona's in '92. I remember all their pools. Of those attending Audubon
Elementary, the lucky had Mrs. Rossi, who took her students to Mosquito Lagoon,

the Cocoa landfill, the water plant, and best of all the woods behind the school—
where the two legs of the island meet (the crotch as You might call it). She

also took us to the swamp. As a class we trudged calf-deep through marsh,
dry in spring, wet in fall. I stepped too far, sinking stomach-deep into the Banana

River. Some kids never left it, dropped down and sleepwalked three miles across
the river-bottom toward Cape Canaveral, cawed at by siren-like stray cats and
    peacocks.

You made me famous in ballet, touring libraries countywide and nursing homes
    at Xmas
time (so You're the X then, right?) for my many roles in Nutcracker: two kinds

of dolls, a candy-cane, a snow flurry, a flower that could waltz, Marzipan, Arabian.
Thank You for them all. Car trips to New Orleans as a kid weren't bad, except I only

had exactly half the back seat to share with my sister (one errant inch, she'd bitch).
I heard *Dark Side of the Moon, Abbey Road*, and now I even like *La Traviata*

and *The Fabulous Baker Boys*. I excavated playground sand to try and get to China.
I thought I reached five feet at least, but probably only two. You kept tabs

on my decisions, like an auger into driftwood, like small holes pinned through
paper scrolls of a player piano. I was a girl scout in third grade, but didn't camp

for fear of bugs. I provided the entertainment; I wowed them with my Steve Urkel impersonation. Mr. Weinbrenner, from down the street, once said you could put me

in the center of a room and not need TV. Before having confidence was a choice, I was so mercurial. My old house is a haunt I dream of nearly nightly. I've seen

unsightly photographs on the internet, the walls now Santa Fe green and Terra Cotta like some Yankee painted it. But when I return it's just the same, white walls

and sliding mirrored closets. My dogs and all my furniture. Whoever bought it for $600,000, I hope I disturb their sleep. The island, You know, wasn't easy

to leave, but harder still to get on. I dreamt a dragon or big dog took a shit at the top of the Hubert Humphrey Bridge—I watched the first approaching cars swerve

and brakes lock. I continued to Cocoa going west, but state road 520 was littered with trash: crashed-looking girls' bikes with rusted bells and daisy baskets.

Two Birds, One Punch

I've never been in a fight but I dream of them
often with girls who've actually pissed
me off. I punch them but can't pound
them. I can't feel their skin on my fists.
When I awake I'm thankful to find my damage
undone. In my dream last night I found the girl
I bit at five, her identity finally, *so* flirting
with Mike. They stood together in some
parking lot—no, the Audubon hardtop.
She said something about juggling his balls
with her tongue probably, and he stared back
with that spitting-game smile. I guess I went
walking really far, like Quincy or something
for auto parts. I approached, punched her jaw
and it actually hurt. *Damn, your history
of attacking me goes back to kindergarten!*
You?   Yeah   Round two
On the pavement we mangled our elbows
and scraped our knees, while Mike and our
P.E. teacher, ever clad in aviators, watched
and drank whiskey—Mr. Beeker from the flask
he had when he taught us, *while* he taught us.
From behind those same sunglasses
he said what he'd say when we ran
on faded asphalt: *You can try to fight
the hardtop   but you won't win.*

Self Portrait as Pinky Driving Down Tropical Trail

Her mom is like the cat
I should go to Alaska
I love smelling things
People with birds are stupid
Sam's birds cried all the damn time
She hated them too
I wish I never had to leave
Too bad this place is fulla rednecks
Hah! it was funny when Joe
Called Mike one—he so is
Grabbing at my tits and shit
How come all the good guys
Never wanna fuck?

Prior Damage

Twice now my roommate fucked up my car,
both times Mike was in on it. In real life
he gave her my keys, and she, rounding
the tight driveway, scraped the driver side
quarter panel—streaks of laser red painted
on the corner of our house. Last night,
in my dream, I found out in dance class—
worst I've ever had. Some 100 people behind
science lab tables with no elbow room.
How're we supposed to move? I scream
and leave to see what she did to my car.
Actually some guy named Enrique
was driving, hit a bump and the engine
sound changed from a purr to a growl
and a warning light, the dollar sign,
blinked on. *Shit*, I thought, *the transmission.*
Her friends stood around my '99 Cougar—
now a convertible since they ripped
off the roof. The hood, more than keyed,
they completely carved into: tribal
shapes and phrases, *Mike Wuz Here*
and *Die With Your Boots On*, edged
with crumpled paint and metal shavings.

Smoking Outside with My Cat on Sunday Morning

On my back porch, a concrete slab surrounded
    by a dirt and pebble driveway,
I arrange a beach chair to get the most sunlight;
    but under trees I have to trade
—my torso in the shade—to tan my face and feet,
    propped on a plant pot. I inhale
with my eyes closed, inside the lids bright red,
    like a baby trying to go back in.
I think about Ben Affleck, how his wife was good
    in *13 Going on 30*, which Megan
recommended, and come up with my own private
    anagram—Panacea Zander.
Now Mike's awake. The door's open and I hear
    as he washes dishes and listens
to Five Blind Boys from Alabama. I think I feel
    the Holy Spirit. Pinky rubs
her whiskers on a flimsy tree—she's going into heat.
    My left eye won't stop crying.
Mike joins me from inside. *Have you eaten yet*
    today, my little angel trumpet?

Pangaea

My name, Panzeca, means dry bread. My whole
life I told my friends I came from bakers.
I swear Mom said they were, a claim she's since
denied. I felt a certain pride when I
baked deli bread: unfurl thawed dough in 10
grooved metal slots, pinholed to let damp air
inflate the yeast in the proofer before
you move the rack to the oven. But once
they cool you have to rip the mass of loaves
apart to bag—rapid plate tectonics
—split again when customers just order
halves. I felt sadness, the lost attachment,
how I imagine the east coast of Flor-
-da remembers its past with Africa.

Frida and Fritz

I've been watching *Frida* a lot and wanna let
my eyebrows grow in naturally like my dad's
always insisted. I've ignored him since
the fourth grade when I shaved with a razor,
disposable plastic, right down the middle
of my faint unibrow, huge two-inch gap,
and still when I look in the yearbook I cringe
but laugh. Last viewing I really heard
what the doctor said happened in the bus
accident: the handrail impaled Frida's side
derecha and came out her vagina. I used
to get menstrual cramps and moan all night,
leave school, pound my fist into walls. Now
I try to enjoy every second of pain
since I know how it feels not to get them
one month. I lied. I just ate a Midol. I've been
watching *Fritz the Cat*, the X-rated cartoon
from the *Hair* era. Viewed with subtitles
en español, when Fritz shouts *Fuck-a-duck!*
(like Mom does) the screen reads *¡Carajo!*
The word, per my Spanish dictionary, means
Damn it all! the very phrase Jessica
would say. Maybe she knows cause her dad's
from El Salvador. Or knew. (That's the good thing
about contractions: *apostrophe s*
can be *is* or *was*.) Her last name's Sandoval,
which her dad said came from an ancestral
warrior, who drew an oval in the sand
(not a sand in the oval). I picture
my parents in New Orleans. They live
in the house Dad grew up in. He stands in front
of the fridge for 15 minutes and asks,
What do they have in here? Mom asks *They?*
I take his arm *izquierda* and walk
him to the sofa. When he gets up
to plod to their bedroom, he clutches his Glock
in one hand, the remote in the other—changes
the station from *White Oleander* to white noise.

His nephew sells him Vicodin. No different
than me smoking weed every day, different
from Jessica only in that he still breathes. Though
he'll die three years later to the day.

[beat]

Enclosed in Hose's Gentle Rain

On Yawl street in Cocoa Beach
where my friend's grandma lived
I used to go as a kid

In the RV parked out front
we'd reenact a scene from *Camp Nowhere*
in which identical twins joke
about blowing up Milwaukee
because their grandma lives there

Inside the house we'd lounge
on antique chairs and shoot pool
on beige felt that matched the carpet

You'd find us in the pool
or dripping chlorine on the patio carpet
one day at a party
we danced our choreography to The Sign
by Ace of Base one night
in a private pact we ate each other's scabs

From the boathouse roof we'd jump into the canal
where I could have swum five brackish miles
diagonally across the Banana River
to my own backyard on Merritt Island
where I'll wait for a friend eight years later
to pick me up in a boat
but he won't have asked his dad
and will have to turn around

From the water we'd climb the metal
mounted ladder no need to plant
our feet on pilings lined with barnacles
slicing our skin as we stand

At the edge of the dock
I'd unscrew the valve
of the garden hose faucet
I'd hold the green rubber above my head
lift my chin to aim my face

at its grooved metal end
the cold water

I forgot about
furniture inside
all that I'd need
is running water
and a knife

and let
pour down my body

the mahogany
and felt
in life
air to gulp
to cut fish

Repose in Light (Feeling Rich Reprise)

You have to walk
brick house on river road
pool water level
exposed on which
the pump broke
the hose and nets
while our host
his parents

behind the big
to see the low
the built-in bench
a moccasin coils
my boyfriend cranks
the baby snake
gets beers
at their other home

I remove my cover-up
until a boat
a mile wide
I stand and drag
I want the passengers
to like my status

self-conscious
in the Indian River
speeds by the house
my cigarette
to want to be me
that is

Until I crouch
on the bench
behind foliage
through blades
eyes at ground level
from the safety

feet submerged
hidden from boats
I peer
at the distant bank
like I'm peeking
of my burrow

I feel like that
who hoards food
or gorges
when I sit
on the dock
I swing my feet
water

ground mammal
for storage
to build fat
under sun
to save warmth
above the brown
minted gold

Gator Takes Travel Cues from Janie and Tea Cake

At my friends' place in West Cocoa
I sit on the back porch overlooking a pond.
A distant rocket readies for launch.

A gator suns himself on a concrete slab
15 feet from me, a screen between us.
He could conceivably climb through the pipe

underneath into the St. Johns River, its mouth
hundreds of miles north—though in a moment,
to the space craft, the distance will collapse.

His grandpa might've done just that, trekked north
to Lake George, inspired Marjorie Kinnan Rawlings,
made a cameo appearance in *The Yearling*.

Or maybe the gator's ancestor preferred
the other Marjory, Stoneman Douglas,
and ventured from this very place I sit

to 13 miles west, the headwaters
of the one and only Everglades.
Then he ambled to Lake Okeechobee

and the Keys to see for himself the *River of Grass*
he'd heard about. All gator generations despise,
like the Marjories did, the onetime majority

view: that Florida's monotonous
wetlands are worthless and undramatic.
Forget Blue Ridges and Yellowstones.

Twenty miles to the northeast, rocket engines
ignite and I ask Mike to block the sun
so I can get a shot. He stands a few moments,

then asks *Did you take the photo yet?*
I'm making a video! He walks away.
The motionless gator recaptures my sight.

Colonial Art

The angle at which you carved,
into magnolia wood, yourself—
Portrait of the Artist—lurching
forward, hand to brow—*Observing
an Indian Maiden at Her Bath*—
I must say, Pierre Joseph Landry,
you look ridiculous. You hunch

only one body length from her back,
arched the same way as she washes
her knee. A single plant the foliage
between. I reread the title in dis-
belief: a self portrait and the pose
is so unflattering. She's bathing,

Pierre. Have you no decency?
In all the time you carved the piece
did you consider a casual stance—
a stolen glance if you must gaze?
Even before you began to cut
did you send your men for chunk
after chunk of fresh magnolia
till you found one that pleased you?

At home I find you fathered 16
children with two wives and more
likely with your slaves. There's
no such thing as a kind master
and you were one of many.

On Turning 30

Someone first borrowed you from my New Orleans
university library in March 1977, two months
after my parents married, 100 years after your author—
Isadora Duncan—'s *Life* began. I read *The Heart
Is a Lonely Hunter* the summer I turned 30. A back page
said McCullers read you (not the very you, a duplicate)
at 14 and was deeply affected. I'm a dancer so of course
I had to find you. Your first chapter, first paragraph,
when your author lived in utero, she says her mother
ate only oysters and champagne, a fact McCullers
might've recalled in 1959. She learned Isak Dinesen
shared the diet just hours before she and Marilyn Monroe
arrived for lunch. 30 years later I was six and Dad set
the box of donuts on the wooden table between
the mantel and the sliding mirror closets. He said *Enjoy these
while you're young. You can't eat anything fun
when you're my age.* But he did anyway. He ate raw oysters
in months without Rs and guzzled them down
with alcohol—a liver-killer recipe (especially
with hep C). But Dad always said that was bullshit.
Thanks to you I know at least two who'd agree.
You stood on metal shelves from 1998 until today,
15 years, *half my life* inside that library unmoved
(maybe save for renovations). Two weeks into your stay
I smoked pot for the first time in some garage
in Port St. John. I always told my parents I wouldn't
move out till I was 35, but they left me in Florida at 18,
three years into your term, to move to the house
in which they were married, not far from your station:
third-floor at the lakefront. Dad would've loved
the constant AC. There to repair units he had panic
attacks in New Orleans attics—antique shops
where he'd see being built what was sold downstairs.
Did you think you'd never come out again?
Halfway through your long repose, deprived yet respited
of sunlight, the bowl below you flooded and many
lost their lives. Nine years after you last left the library
Dad died of a heart attack. To everyone's surprise

he almost made 30 twice. Three months shy. *A young man*
we all said. In case you're never checked out again
I'm bringing you to California, your author's birthplace.
Like her I'm most alive by the sea. My first time
at the beach after 30 was in Mississippi. I only
went in to my knees. I waded in that same water
six days from 28. Amy Winehouse, same age,
died that morning. I wasn't in danger now of joining
the 27-club with her and Kurt Cobain. I was 10
when he died and didn't see him then as such a young
man. My last week of my twenties I was back
on Cocoa Beach. My baby nephew from Alaska
splashed in the ocean for the first time. I smoked
joints with Mom on walks in the sand and fell
creatively into waves like Isadora must have.

[beat]

The Infinite Santa Monica Sand

I had no interest in Los Angeles, until I saw
every place name I'd ever heard in movies on one map.

Because of scenes I'd seen on screen, I didn't believe
(when someone told me) the ocean is too cold to swim.

When I visited Santa Monica, I had to stick my big toe
in. From the clean streets, where homeless people slept,

I descended the steps down the palisades;
trudged 300 calf-crunching steps

across the wide beach. My shoes, made of basket-like jute,
collected thousands of grains—unintentional souvenirs.

In a diner bathroom, I beat my flats against a wall
above a trashcan. Out fell cupfuls of sand.

Even now, months removed, I find grains
on my toes after wearing those shoes.

A science teacher once asked my class,
to help us grasp the smallness of atoms,

to picture ourselves on a plane looking down
at the beach. If we'd never set foot in sand,

and saw that strip of tan, imagine our shock
at hearing it's made of billions of grains.

If I captured pieces of that beach,
did I leave behind some of me?

Lean

A swing set on the beach, or heaven. I lean toward the ocean, chest between chains, elbows poised behind to punch or fly, knees curled under. Toes hide until they snake and sweep and nearly graze the sand and reach for the Pacific. Biceps pull the metal links, torso in a plane like in a bed or grave. I repeat like ocean waves, but only move a body length. Get me higher, swing. My eyes climb the chain—must be 20 feet. Impossibility springs. Something about fulcrums. I give up. Muscle Beach? Pshaw. Joke's on me.

We gravitate to the swings after renting movies we won't end up watching from the mountain cabin office. I debate which seat to take and which way to face; I don't want to see road below. There's real danger I'll let go—last night a guy with altitude sickness, and footlong sideburns, pitched headlong into the log bench on which I sat. I sink into the strap, tattered burlap, giving Mike, six-two, the bigger black plastic. He flips it over, undoing my work, and sees what I saw: bird poop. Soon we're high but every time we pull or push our chains, the ancient frame creaks louder. Would I notice the sensation right away if the whole jalopy tumbled down the road? What about the mountain? The seat's U squeezes my hips. I quit.

At 7:10, every day, I'd line up first by the back door of the daycare, where Mom worked, to play. Fingertips and breath behind me—Blast—through the door I'd power-walk (no running) on concrete and in sand, and just before the fence and scrub, I'd reach the first swing's rut, claim the chains above, and twirl my rump into the rung. I'd lean, fore and aft on repeat, until prompted by the intercom to walk to school across the street. Palms smelled of rust till lunch.

Public Nudity

The California Heritage Museum
to my back, I wait to cross the street.
A woman stands facing me
and the block-away beach, wearing
a tankini top that reaches her
low waist. My eyes aren't good. I think
there has to be more fabric.

As my boyfriend and I walk
to her side of the street, I see labia
grazed with a week of hair—less than
my own. I look up, she glares.

This is the stuff of stressful dreams:
bottomless in public and too late
to go home. Next I'll see toilets in stalls
with walls too low, seats with rims
too thin around bowls too big,
and yards of pipe like water slides
leaving scant leg room. At three

in my Florida front yard, surrounded
by lawn on my little island of mulch
between two palms, I stood—
maybe on the coquina rock—
wearing only a white tee. No one told
me yet it wasn't okay. I even
waved to neighbors.

Property Values

The neighbors douse their lawns to conform
(heteronormative *lawn order*) to ideals
I associate with Donna Reed
and date rape. At least in the '50s
the Indian River Lagoon was healthy.
Few people lived there. Dikes built
to kill mosquitoes crushed cleansing
wetlands. Damned fluidity. Gutted
the riparian spectrum (a lamebow left
with red and violet). Extinguished species
for whom the need for fluctuation's
not a luxury (r.i.p. dusky sea-
side sparrow). All for a dry-flood binary
enforced because skeeter eggs need both
to soak and sunbathe. With water just
water and land firmly land all things flow
only one way. Fertilizer washes down
with every rain, inundates the lagoon
with nitrogen and phosphorus. Algae blooms
and superblooms, hogs the oxygen
sea grass and fish need to live.
Dead dolphins and pelicans,
hundreds, found with empty
stomachs. Dozens of dead
manatees, stomachs full
but made for grass, fouled
with macroalgae. They eat
what they can. Tumors form
under skins. It rains nearly
every day in summer.
Each drop, each drop—
Each drop, each drop—
more runoff
more chemicals.
The waterway
may be headed
from the most bio-
diverse estuary

in North America
to total devastation.
But damn
if those aren't
some pretty lawns.

Where's the Tree?

Black seeds that coat my ankles came from V-
topped weeds—the grass impossible to mow
enough in summer. The sun behind me
warms my back and casts a shaft that traces
the length of the thousand-space parking lot
and lands high on a brick wall a smatter
of fronds, tall like a California palm.
Nearby a clump of scraggly Sabals hunch,
short with fronds that flail and sag. The shadow's
neat and singular, and from that angle—
Over my right shoulder I see, planted
in acres of asphalt, a rusted trunk
that inches up a hundred feet to reach
a circumference of eight branching floodlights.

Essayons

I righted it   to legs again   again it wronged
to back   I want to call it *him*   I drove home
from dance class   and in the driveway   found him
still mid-attempt   legs still trying   to scuttle the sky
top two like claws   bottom four long   maybe a cicada
I propped him up   with a dry leaf   I grabbed from under
the Satsuma tree   ants scurried   from gnawing
his body   I blew to scram   the more persistent
he dragged his head   thorax   abdomen
and legs   lame on one side   in a wide arc
until he rolled   onto his chewed   but armored back
I went inside   to get Mom   I said it wasn't
fair   she said   *his life's just over*
that night   I saw concentric waves   in the pool
their source   a fluttering black spot   I thought
about the driveway bug   who'd probably   long
stopped kicking   half his body gone   I reached for the net
remembered when   I scooped in cupped hands   a drowning bee
who stung me   as water leaked   through my fingers
a friend laughed   that I called it   an *asshole*
then stopped myself   *look first*   I stepped
in faded light   to the edge of the pool   peered through
humid dusk   near-opacity   to see a water beetle

Floating in the Pool

The trick to floating is to lift
your chin, to submit to the sky,
and not worry if water slips
into your ears. I never was
one of those people who
pinched their nose as they jumped
in. It's easiest with lungs full
of air—legs first to go limp
on the exhale. You won't fall
to the bottom if you hold on
a little longer, till the next time
you inhale, I swear.

If the pool somehow flipped I'd fall
like rain, or more like a toad: in one
piece. Gravity: the only rule of water
that matters to me. Each molecule
torturous if dripped by the drop
on a forehead. Under the rain gutter,
where the deck meets the porch,
after every storm, there's a little less
of the Chattahoochee rock
you can't get anymore.

I have the time to calculate
the depth of pool water if emptied
into my house—two inches
above the baseboard? Six?
But then I'd have to subtract
the displacement of furniture
and pets. I don't want a Eureka
moment right now. A teacher
might use my floating body
to illustrate surface tension:

I'm bulging from the bowl,
here a knee, here a nose,
a marginal world—not land
or sea—a beach. I'm peering
out through a screen, or from
the chamber of a shell. The om
of the pool pump the only sound.

Notes

Page 4   *"Self Portrait as Pinky Driving Down Tropical Trail"*
A character sketch for the protagonist of a short story, loosely based on my cat, Pinky, who at the time lived with a neutered male cat, Nico, who offered no relief when she was in heat.

Page 7   *how I imagine the east coast of Flor- / -da remembers its past with Africa*
"Geologists have found rock patterns below Senegal and Sierra Leone that match rock patterns below Florida like the two sides of a ripped dollar bill." Michael Grunwald. *The Swamp: The Everglades, Florida, and the Politics of Paradise*. New York: Simon, 2006. 374.

Page 12   *Enclosed in Hose's Gentle Rain*
"The days are bright and filled with pain / Enclose me in your gentle rain." The Doors. "The Crystal Ship." *The Doors*, 1967.

Page 13   *all that I'd need   in life*
"I never thought that I would find / All that I need in life." Soul for Real. "Candy Rain." *Candy Rain*, 1994.

Page 14   *Repose in Light*
"'Repose in light can be—tends to be—peace through light, light that appeases and gives peace; but repose in light is also repose—deprivation of all external help and impetus—so that nothing comes to disturb, or to pacify, the pure movement of the light. ... *Repose in light*: is it sweet appeasement through light? Is it the difficult deprivation of oneself and of all of one's own movement, a position in the light without repose? Here two infinitely different experiences are separated by almost nothing.'" Maurice Blanchot quoted by Mary Ruefle. "Poetry and the Moon." *Madness, Rack, and Honey*. Seattle: Wave Books, 2012. 30.

Page 15   *Gator Takes Travel Cues from Janie and Tea Cake*
For more on how Zora Neale Hurston uses Florida geography in her novel, see "Naturalism and the Florida Setting in *Their Eyes Were Watching God* by Zora Neale Hurston." Andrea Panzeca. <http://www.ualberta.ca/~aizen/excavatio/archives/v24.html>

Page 15   *gator generations despise, / like the Marjories did, the onetime*
                        majority / / view
Thanks also to Marjorie Harris Carr for leading the successful effort to stop the
Cross Florida Barge Canal.

Page 16   Portrait of the Artist […] / […] Observing / an Indian
                        Maiden at Her Bath
Magnolia woodcut by Pierre Joseph Landry viewed at New Orleans Museum
of Art.

Page 16   *till you found one that pleased you?*
Inspired by Jody Stark, who "sent men out to the swamp to cut the finest and
straightest cypress post they could find, and kept sending them back to hunt
another one until they found one that pleased him." Hurston. *Their Eyes Were
Watching God*. New York: Harper, 2006. 44.

Page 17   *Someone first borrowed you*
Isadora Duncan's *My Life*. New York: Boni and Liveright, 1928.

Page 20   *From the clean streets, where homeless people slept*
When recording *Le Show* from Santa Monica Harry Shearer calls it "the home
for the homeless."

Page 23   *(heteronormative …*
Inspired by "deductive reasoning joke" whereby Boudreaux correctly deduces
Thibodeaux has a house, wife, and kids because he has a lawnmower, but then
(presumably incorrectly) deduces Robichaux is gay because he doesn't have
one.
                … lawn order)
"*Law and order* could be seen as starting from *lawn order*, valued by so many
Americans." Lydia Davis. "A Mown Lawn." 2001.

Page 23   *Dikes built / to kill mosquitoes crushed cleansing / wetlands*
"By creating permanent impoundments behind the dikes, the entire salt marsh
flooding regimen was transformed. The broomgrass could not withstand
constant flooding and was replaced by thick shrubs. Impounding also changed
the salt marsh to mostly fresh water, as the brackish Indian and Banana Rivers
were kept at bay and rain filled the impoundments. This change to fresh water
encouraged the growth of cattails. The cattails and shrubby growth, in turn,

ushered in their own animal clientele. The heretofore scarce red-winged blackbird became common on Merritt Island, as did the aggressive boat-tailed grackle. The land of broomgrass and open salt marsh became a series of shallow, stagnant freshwater ponds." Mark Jerome Walters. *A Shadow and A Song: The Struggle to Save an Endangered Species*. White River Junction, VT: Chelsea Green Publishing, 2007. 31–32.

Page 23   *skeeter eggs need both / to soak and sunbathe*
"Mosquitoes laid their eggs in the mud of the broomgrass flats surrounding the island exposed at low tide. The eggs incubated for three days, and then after a high tide or rain, hatched to liberate the larvae, which took flight as adults a week later. From spring through fall, with high tides or rain often following dry periods, the mosquitoes were at their worst. After a heavy rain, a single acre of Merritt Island salt marsh could produce fifty million mosquitoes." ibid. 25.

Page 23   *Each drop, each drop— / Each drop, each drop—*
Inspired by: "And you, and you— / And you, and you—" Suji Kwock Kim. "Occupation." *Notes from the Divided Country: Poems*. Baton Rouge: LSU Press, 2003. 19.

Page 26   Essayons
essay (noun, verb): to attempt or try
Essayons ("Let us try"): motto of the US Army Corps of Engineers

$\mathbf{A}$ndrea Panzeca graduated from the University of New Orleans with an M.F.A. in Creative Writing and Florida State University with a B.A. in Creative Writing. Her awards include a Pabst Cultural Endowment Scholarship to attend Residency #159 at the Atlantic Center for the Arts and the Carol Gelderman Award for Nonfiction Thesis in 2015, the Andrea Saunders Gereighty/Academy of American Poets Poetry Award in 2013, and the UNO Vassar Miller Poetry Award in 2013 and 2012. Her poetry and prose have appeared in *Ellipsis* and her scholarly essay "Naturalism and the Florida Setting in *Their Eyes Were Watching God* by Zora Neale Hurston" appeared in *Excavatio* vol. XXIV. She is a former associate nonfiction editor at *Bayou Magazine*. She recently served as a panelist on creating comics (graphic narratives) at the Other Words Conference in St. Augustine, and is training to become a Louisiana Master Naturalist in New Orleans. She grew up in Merritt Island, Florida.

www.ingramcontent.com/pod-product-compliance
Lightning Source LLC
LaVergne TN
LVHW091234080426
835509LV00009B/1283